SHARK SEARCH

In Search of
Blue Sharks

Seth Dempski

PowerKiDS
press™

New York

Published in 2016 by The Rosen Publishing Group, Inc.
29 East 21st Street, New York, NY 10010

First Edition

Editor: Caitie McAneney
Book Design: Mickey Harmon

Photo Credits: Cover (iron bars) Wayne Lynch/All Canada Photos/Getty Images; cover, pp. 1, 3, 4, 6, 8, 10, 12, 14, 16, 18, 20–24 (background) Ase/Shutterstock.com; cover (blue shark), p. 17 Cultura Science/Richard Robinson/Cultura Exclusive/Getty Images; pp. 5, 11, 22 Dray van Beeck/Shutterstock.com; p. 7 Cultura RM/George Karbus Photography/Cultura/Getty Images; pp. 9, 13 Westend61/Getty Images; p. 14 bochimsang12/Shutterstock.com; p. 15 marina durante/Shutterstock.com; p. 19 Shane Gross/Shutterstock.com; p. 20 Joost van Uffelen/Shutterstock.com.

Cataloging-in-Publication Data

Dempski, Seth.
In search of blue sharks / by Seth Dempski.
p. cm. — (Shark search)
Includes index.
ISBN 978-1-5081-4331-4 (pbk.)
ISBN 978-1-5081-4332-1 (6-pack)
ISBN 978-1-5081-4333-8 (library binding)
1. Blue shark — Juvenile literature. I. Dempski, Seth. II. Title.
QL638.95.C3 D465 2016
597.3'4—d23

Manufactured in the United States of America

CPSIA Compliance Information: Batch #BW16PK: For Further Information contact Rosen Publishing, New York, New York at 1-800-237-9932

Contents

Beautiful Blue Biters

Blue sharks are known as some of the most beautiful and graceful sharks in the sea. However, don't think they're all beauty and no bite. These sharks are tough predators that can put up a fight!

Blue sharks get their name from the blue color of their skin. They're also called blue dogs and blue pointers. Their coloring makes them easy to **identify**. However, you may have to go to the deep sea to find a blue shark.

You may wonder why you've never seen a blue shark in an aquarium. That's because these sharks can only survive in the wild.

Swimming the Open Sea

The search for a blue shark starts with the open sea. This shark is found in all ocean waters around the world except for **Arctic** waters. It likes cool water, but will swim in warm waters, too.

Blue sharks generally hunt around 1,312 feet (400 m) under the water's surface. That's the deep sea! Blue sharks sometimes swim closer to the surface, too. They swim in open waters and **migrate** long distances for food.

Blue sharks are known to jump right out of the water to find **prey** on the surface!

Torpedo Bodies

Blue sharks have a thin body and a pointed **snout**. They're shaped like a **torpedo**. That makes it easy to cut through water. The blue shark has several fins to help it swim. The caudal fin is part of its tail, while the dorsal fin is on top of its body. The pectoral fins are on each side.

How can you identify a blue shark? Look at its color. It's no surprise that blue sharks have blue skin, which is lighter on their underside.

Blue sharks can grow to about 13 feet (4 m) long. They're pretty light for a shark, only weighing around 450 pounds (204 kg).

dorsal fin

caudal fin

pectoral fins

Excellent Senses

Blue sharks are set apart from other sharks in many ways. However, most sharks share the same helpful supersenses.

People usually can see, smell, hear, taste, and feel. Blue sharks have all those senses, but they can also sense electric fields in the water. All living things give off an electric field through their muscle movements, even their heartbeat. A blue shark is able to pick up on a heartbeat that's happening miles away! That helps it hunt for its prey.

Blue sharks have large eyes. They have a great sense of sight, even in the deep sea.

Living in Schools

Most shark species, or kinds, live and hunt alone. However, blue sharks like to stick together. Groups of fish are called "schools," and so are groups of blue sharks. These sharks are sometimes called "wolves of the sea," because wolves live and hunt in groups, too.

Blue sharks swim in male-only and female-only groups. They usually swim with sharks of the same size. Males and females stay separate most of the time, except for **mating**.

Blue sharks rely on teamwork to catch a big meal.

Predators of the Deep

The blue shark may be a graceful swimmer, but it's also a wild predator. Blue shark schools wander the ocean looking for any food they can find.

A blue shark's favorite meal is squid. Because they like this slippery treat, they have many rows of teeth to grab hold of it. Blue sharks also eat small fish and other sharks, as well as sea birds and lobster. Because they'll eat anything, they're called "opportunistic feeders."

squid

14

Blue sharks are considered scavengers because they'll eat things other creatures often won't. Scavengers are important parts of ocean **ecosystems** because they feed on dead animals.

Blue Shark Babies

Male and female blue sharks rarely meet, but they do come together to mate. Female blue sharks have skin that's three times thicker than males' skin because males tend to bite females quite hard.

Most fish lay eggs, but the blue shark is different. After 9 to 12 months, the female blue shark gives birth to live babies, which are called pups. She can have between 5 and 130 pups at a time! Once the pups are born, the mother leaves.

The bigger a mother blue shark is, the more pups she can have.

Are Blue Sharks Dangerous?

Blue sharks aren't interested in hunting people. However, it's still good to be safe in waters known to have blue sharks. Blue sharks don't usually attack humans when they're left alone. However, fishermen have been attacked while trying to catch a blue shark.

There are only about a dozen blue shark attacks on record that weren't **provoked**. If you see a blue shark while swimming, it's important to leave it alone and swim away.

Divers need to be careful when they come face-to-face with a blue shark. These sharks may be beautiful, but their strong jaws and sharp teeth make them **dangerous**!

19

Overfishing the Blue Shark

The blue shark might be fast and strong, but it's no match for humans. People fish for blue sharks more than any other shark in the world. Between 10 million and 20 million blue sharks are killed every year.

Why do people kill blue sharks? People take the skin and jaws of the shark to sell. They take the fins for a special soup. People also kill these sharks for the oil in their liver.

Shark Bites!

 A blue shark's predators include killer whales, great white sharks, and tiger sharks.

 A blue shark usually lives for around 20 years.

 Blue sharks can swim over 20 miles (32 km) per hour and even faster in short bursts.

 If a blue shark loses teeth, new teeth move forward to fill the space.

 The **organs** a blue shark uses to sense electrical fields are called the ampullae of Lorenzini.

 Blue sharks are sometimes known to swim in circles around divers and swimmers.

Saving the Blue Shark

Today, the beautiful blue shark is considered threatened, which means it's at risk of dying out. Their populations are dropping each year due to overfishing. People also pollute the ocean water blue sharks call home. Blue sharks sometimes eat garbage and litter in the ocean, which can kill them.

How can we save the blue shark? Lawmakers can pass laws to **protect** the blue shark. People can help cut down on pollution. Most importantly, you can tell others all about the blue shark!

Glossary

Arctic: The area around the North Pole that's very cold.

dangerous: Unsafe.

ecosystem: All the living things in an area.

identify: To tell what something is.

mate: To come together to make babies.

migrate: To move from one area to another for feeding or having babies.

organ: A body part that does a certain task.

prey: An animal hunted by other animals for food.

protect: To keep safe.

provoke: To bother or make angry.

snout: An animal's nose and mouth.

torpedo: A rocket-shaped exploding device that travels through water.

Index

Websites

Due to the changing nature of Internet links, PowerKids Press has developed an online list of websites related to the subject of this book. This site is updated regularly. Please use this link to access the list: www.powerkidslinks.com/search/blue